Text copyright © 2013 Carmen Martinez Jover
www.carmenmartinezjover.com
Illustrations copyright © 2014 Rosemary Martinez
www.rosemarymartinezartdesign.com.mx

ISBN: 978-607-00-8397-6

Somy's Search, a single Mum by choice story
1st edition November 2014

Written by: Carmen Martinez Jover
Illustrated by: Rosemary Martinez
Collaborators: Abelardo, Mary Carmen Zepeda & Victor Nieto

Special thanks to:
Sandra K Dill A, CEO, Access Australia www.access.org.au
Chair, iCSi patient communitywww.icsicommunity.org
Sandra de la Garza, founder, www.ami-ac.com, author "Cuando tarda la Cigüeña"
(When the Stork is Delayed)
Rosa Maestro, founder, www.masola.org, author "Cloe quiere ser Mama"
(Cloe wants to be a Mum)

I dedicate this story
with all my admiration to all
those single Mums by choice
who dance with love to the
daily rhythm of life to bring up
their children.
Carmen

Dedicated to all those
who dare to strive
for their dreams.
Rosemary

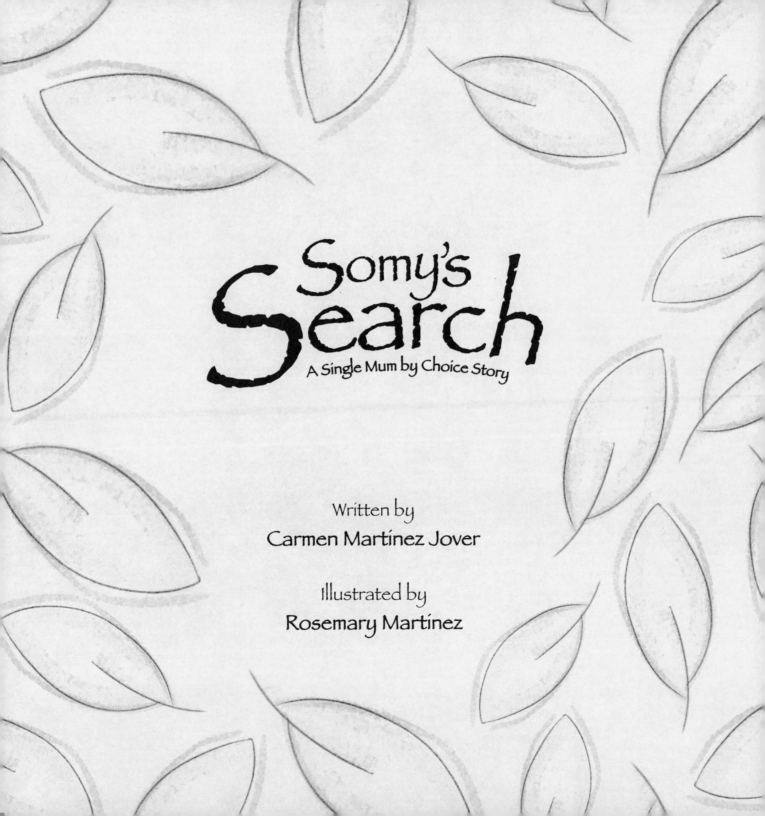

Somy's Search

A Single Mum by Choice Story

Written by

Carmen Martínez Jover

Illustrated by

Rosemary Martínez

Once upon a time there was a clever and friendly squirrel called Somy. She was named after Somilge, the Goddess of Magic.

She lived in a cosy tree which she had decorated to her taste.

7

Somy loved children and she wanted to have one of her own.

9.

One evening, as Somy and
her neighbour Doris,
were tidying the house
after celebrating Somy's
birthday, Somy said:

"I'm getting older, Doris, and
I really want to have my own
baby squirrel. I feel time is
catching up on me."

10

"Well, you need to try and
meet someone you like,"
replied Doris.

11

12

So Somy started
looking for this
special person and
she met:

Huggy Hedgehog
and
Charming Chihuahua...

13

and
Geeky Goose

and
Funny Fox...

14

"Oh Doris, I'm so tired, I met lots of possible partners but none of them have conquered my heart. And not one that I thought could be a good Dad either," said Somy.

"I am worried, Doris, I feel that I am growing too old to have a baby, and that if I wait any longer then I might never be able to have a child."

"Well," said Doris, "you're right, as time goes by your eggs and womb get older and the chances of you falling pregnant get smaller.

Why don't you find a sperm from a donor?"

17

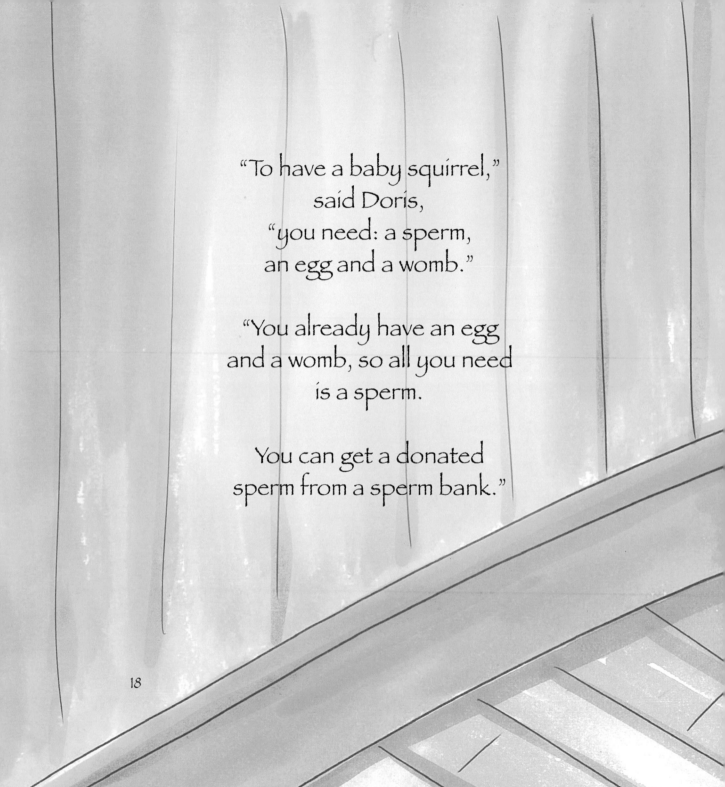

"To have a baby squirrel,"
said Doris,
"you need: a sperm,
an egg and a womb."

"You already have an egg
and a womb, so all you need
is a sperm.

You can get a donated
sperm from a sperm bank."

a sperm

an egg

a womb

a baby squirrel

So off went Somy Squirrel
to visit Dr. Amare who
opened the sperm bank
and gave Somy a sperm.

21

In the clinic, Dr. Amare gently put
Somy's egg and the donated sperm
together in a test tube and patiently
looked after them until they fertilised
and became one, forming an embryo,
which is the beginning of a baby.

When the embryo started to grow,
Dr. Amare placed it carefully
into Somy Squirrel's womb,
where it continued...

growing... and growing...
and growing.

24

and then in Somy's womb,
the little baby squirrel
continued growing....
and grow... and grow!.

Somy's friends and family were so excited about her pregnancy that they organised a baby shower for little baby squirrel!

At last Somy
became a Mummy!

Little baby squirrel was born!
Such a beautiful and desired baby squirrel!
Together they became
a very happy family!

28

Other books by
Carmen & Rosemary Martinez Jover

Purchase at:
www.amazon.com
www.carmenmartinezjover.com

I want to have a child,
Whatever it takes!

Recipes of How
Babies are Made

A tiny itsy bitsy gift of life,
an egg donor story: girls, boys*

The Twin Kangaroo
Treasure Hunt*

The Twin Kangaroo
Treasure Hunt: twins*

* Available in:
English, Español, Français, Italiano,
Português, Svenska, Türkiye, Česky, Русский & Nederlands

Lightning Source UK Ltd.
Milton Keynes UK
UKRC012216100320
360130UK00007B/32